Shredding It

A Cabbage Cookbook

Volume Two in the "Brassbright Cooks" Series

Lori Alden Holuta

Edited by Ken Holuta

Author's cover photo courtesy of John-Michael O'Brien at PhotoNinjas.net

Graphic Credits: Vintage graphics used throughout this cookbook are in the public domain. Many of them were curated by The Graphics Fairy (thegraphicsfairy.com), a delightful website you should visit and support.

For more information or media inquiries, email lori@ceejaywriter.com

I'm dedicating this cookbook to my favorite celebrity chefs and foodies! They have inspired, instructed, and entertained me throughout the years. Some of them I've loved since I was a kid baking tiny cakes in my Kenner Easy-Bake Oven.

Julia Child • James May • Duff Goldman • Alton Brown
Anthony Bourdain • Phil Rosenthal • Jacques Pépin
Jon Favreau • Bobby Flay • Guy Fieri • Max Miller
Valerie Bertinelli • Martin Yan • Emeril Lagasse
Mario Batali • Graham Kerr • Samin Nosrat

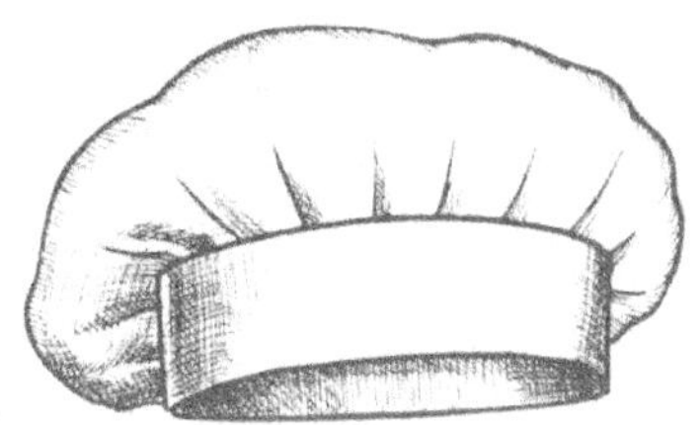

Contents

"Let them fart fire and brimstone... I will not have a single case of scurvy on my hands, the sea-surgeon's shame, while there is cabbage to be culled."

Patrick O'Brian's 1978 novel, *Desolation Island*

"In the 1700s it was found that sauerkraut (fermented cabbage) could prevent the deadly scurvy that killed many sailors on long sea voyages."

South Dakota State University Extension Website

But Lori, Why Cabbage?

This cookbook is the result of inventing a fictional holiday called "Greensday", which is celebrated by characters in a novel I'm writing called *Down the Tubes*. When my characters get hungry, I often feed them something from my recipe collection. When I realized that the official vegetable of Greensday was going to be cabbage, I knew it was only a matter of time before I'd give in and create a cabbage cookbook. And here we are. *Shredding It* is my second cookbook, and I suspect it won't be my last.

Measuring Up

My recipe collection reflects my upbringing in the United States. If you live elsewhere, you may need to convert temperatures to Celsius and the measurements to your own local standards.

1-2-3 Cook!

Always read a recipe *three times* before you start. First, read to see if this is a dish you'll enjoy making. Second, read to be sure you have all the ingredients and equipment needed. Third, read to understand the preparation and cooking methods.

Cabbage is a New Cook's Best Friend

If you've never whacked a knife into a mighty head of green cabbage, you can relax. It's hard to go wrong. Cabbage is *very* forgiving.

Even if you use too much or too little, chop it too fine or too coarse, you're still going to have a delicious dish. If you bake it too long it will probably just develop extra flavor.

This cookbook focuses on tried-and-true comfort recipes that don't require expert skills. Most of them are the everyday dishes our grandparents might have enjoyed.

And Now a Word from the Lawyers

Cooking and baking involves inherent danger. Sharp tools and high heat are often a part of the preparation process.

You may be allergic to certain foods. The author cannot know your personal skill level or dietary restrictions. It's up to you to use common sense and care when preparing these recipes.

The author is not responsible for any accidents or personal harm resulting from the preparation of food using the recipes and instructions in this book. These recipes are to be used at your own risk.

To Index or Not to Index

I decided not to include a traditional index in the back of this cookbook. The nature of these recipes means that many of the ingredients are common to many of the recipes.

An index would have ended up being huge, listing almost every recipe under almost every ingredient! With that much redundancy, an index ceases to be helpful. And I'll be honest; creating an index is hard work, which I don't mind doing if it's helpful, but this time, the payoff is just too small.

Instead, I encourage you to simply flip through the cookbook and skim the recipes until you find one that suits your needs.

The author, relaxing while her cabbage rolls steam

Reviving Retro Recipes

The recipes in this book are from my own collection, and also contributed by my foodie friends and family. Some recipes were handed down through generations, while others are modern.

The further back in time you go, the greater the chance is that a recipe will assume you already know various things without actually mentioning them. Cooking temperatures, size and type of cookware, and the amounts of simple ingredients such as water and salt are often omitted. I'm not fond of assumptions, so I've added 'assumed' ingredients and instructions back into these recipes.

My Mom Called It Something Else!

Some of these recipes may have names that are close to, but not quite what you were expecting. With recipes passed down through generations, and carried from country to country, recipe names are sometimes changed or even misspelled.

Often, I've added to my collection by complimenting a cook and asking for the recipe. I usually come home with a container of leftovers and a hastily scrawled recipe, written by the cook from memory. That's one way that recipe ingredients change over time. Another way is substitutions that are made to accommodate dietary needs, or just to appeal to different taste buds. You have my blessing to grab a sharpie and 'correct' your copy of this cookbook as you see fit. I've included 'pages at the end of each section for you to scribble on, but you can write on the recipe pages too!

Opening a Can of Confusion

The size of cans has changed significantly over time. This may be a problem when trying to decipher heirloom recipes. In general, a "large can" of, shall we say sauerkraut since this is a cabbage cookbook, typically refers to a can that's approximately 28 to 32 ounces. However, if you're unsure, you could hold back a portion  of the can's contents at first, and add them later to suit your personal preferences, if needed. You can always put more in, but you can't take too much back out.

Here's a list of the most commonly referred to can sizes, which may appear in recipes up through the 1980s.

No. 1 (Picnic) 1-1/4 cups	No. 300 1 ¾ cups	No. 303 & No. 1 Tall 2 cups
No. 2 2-1/2 cups	No. 2-1/2 3-1/2 cups	No. 3 4 cups
No. 5 7-1/4 cups	No. 10 13 cups	(Space for you to add one!)

The "Soup Can" Situation

Store-bought cans of condensed tomato soup are a common ingredient in cabbage recipes. But I make my own 'copycat' condensed, no-sodium tomato soup and can it in pint jars to better suit our diet. So, we home-canners need to know how many cups there are in a 'can'.

A regular can of Campbell's tomato soup is 10.75 ounces. That's about 1-1/3 cups.

Heinz tomato soup comes in various sizes, but their 'regular' can is 13.2 ounces, which works out to just a little more than 1-1/2 cups.

Luckily, I have not found a cabbage recipe yet that requires an *exact* measurement of tomato soup. If you're somewhere in the ballpark, you'll be just fine.

Oleo-Oh-No! Outdated Ingredients

I've done my best to convert older ingredient references throughout this cookbook to understandable modern-day wording. You know you've found a vintage recipe if it calls for oleo, hamburg, or shortening. I've assembled a chart on the next page explaining some of the questionable ingredients I've run across through the years.

Old Ingredient Substitution Suggestions

Aspic: Savory meat-flavored gelatin. Meats and vegetables suspended in aspic used to be wildly popular. Add unflavored gelatin to beef, poultry or pork soup stock.

Candied Peel: Use candied citrus zest.

Corn Syrup: A sugary syrup made from corn starches. Replace with honey, maple syrup, or liquid sweeteners.

Currant Jelly: Substitute grape jelly or other fruit preserves.

Drippings: Fats rendered from meat. Use vegetable oil.

Frumenty: Very old word for porridge or oatmeal.

Hamburg: It's just ground beef.

Lard: Solid animal fat that has been separated from the meat. Substitute oil, butter, or margarine.

Mace: A spice that comes from the shell of the nutmeg nut. It's stronger and spicier than nutmeg, so add a dash of black pepper if you are substituting nutmeg for mace.

Oleo: Just an old term for margarine.

Rennet: Enzymes from young mammal's stomach linings. Can be ordered from cheesemaking supply outlets. Vegetarian substitutes also exist.

Rosewater: It's lovely if you can find or make some, otherwise vanilla extract may be substituted.

Saleratus: Sodium bicarbonate (or sometimes potassium bicarbonate) is the main ingredient in baking powder, so just use baking powder.

Shortening: Any fat that is solid at room temperature. Substitutes can be oil, butter, or margarine.

Suet: The hard, raw fat removed from around the kidneys and loins of beef, lamb, or mutton. Substitute oil, butter, or margarine.

Sweetmeats: Not actually meat! It's candied fruit or nuts.

Upcycling Vintage Recipes

If you want to honor traditional cooking while still pleasing modern palates, here are some ideas for bringing an old recipe up the timeline and into modern kitchens.

Reduce Sodium and Fat: Many (okay, most) older recipes tend to be heavy on salt and fat. Cut way back on the amount of salt called for or use a salt substitute. Switch to healthier fats such as olive or avocado oil instead of shortening, butter, bacon grease, or lard.

Incorporate Vegetables: Older recipes often place the emphasis on meat and starches. Adding vegetables can increase the nutritional value and make them taste better.

Make it Vegetarian: Consider using ingredients like tofu, tempeh, lentils, and beans as substitutes for meat.

Experiment with Global Flavors: Simple twists like adding sriracha for a spicy kick or soy sauce and ginger can give a dish some worldly sophistication.

Substitute Healthier Ingredients: Think about using whole wheat flour instead of white flour, Greek yogurt instead of sour cream, or honey instead of sugar.

Simplify Cooking Methods: Update complex cooking techniques with an air fryer or your Instant Pot.

Use Seasonal Ingredients: Fresh, in-season produce not only enhances flavor and nutritional value but can also help support your local farmers.

Presentation: Brighten a dish by garnishing it with fresh herbs, colorful vegetables, or edible flowers.

Cabbage-Centric Recipe Revamps

Explore Other Cabbage Varieties: Cabbage isn't always a round green ball. Substitute red, Napa, or Savoy cabbage. Each variety has its own unique flavor and texture.

Experiment with Cooking Methods: So many older cabbage recipes take place in a frying pan or casserole dish. Roasting, grilling, sautéing, or braising can also get the job done, and might even result in better flavor and texture.

Add Protein: Incorporate plant-based protein sources, such as tofu, tempeh, beans, lentils, and chickpeas, into your cabbage recipes to make them more satisfying and nutritious.

Experiment with Sauces and Dressings: Homemade sauces and dressings add flavor and depth. Consider making a tangy peanut sauce for a cabbage salad or a spicy sriracha glaze to drizzle on roasted cabbage wedges.

Shake Up the Side Dishes: Instead of mashed potatoes or rice, consider pairing cabbage with quinoa, farro, or cauliflower rice for a modern twist.

Add Texture: We can't change the fact that cabbage goes soft when cooked. Add back some crunch with nuts, seeds, or even crispy tofu.

Have Fun! Cooking should be enjoyable and creative. You just might be the one to come up with a new recipe to pass on to the next generation.

Weird Cabbage Trivia

 French explorer Jacques Cartier claimed what is now Canada in the name of France. But of more importance to foodies, he's responsible for bringing cabbage to the New World in 1541.

In World War I, the British wrapped the feet of trench foot patients in cabbage leaves. They were thought to have 'cooling' properties.

"Cabbage Patch Kids" were inspired by actual cabbages. The dolls were designed to look like newborns peeking out from cabbage leaves.

The word "cabbage" is an Anglicized version of the French word *caboche*, which means "head."

Babe Ruth wore a cabbage leaf under his baseball cap during baseball games. It's been said that he switched it out for a fresh leaf halfway through the game.

In 1982, cabbage seeds were grown in orbit aboard the Space Shuttle Columbia. This experiment was performed to examine the effects of microgravity on plant growth. The cabbage didn't do well. It was stressed, and they concluded that it was sensitive to continuously elevated CO_2 levels.

In 2012, at the annual Giant Cabbage Weigh-Off, Scott Robb of Palmer, Alaska submitted a cabbage that set the record with a weight of 138.25 pounds. That's a LOT of slaw.

APPETIZERS

'Flowering' Cabbage

Inspired by a certain restaurant's iconic fried onion.

1-1/2 cups all-purpose flour
1-1/2 cups cornstarch
2 tbsp salt
2 tbsp powdered garlic
2 tbsp ground cumin
2 tbsp smoked paprika
1 tbsp dried thyme
2 tsp dried oregano
2 tsp cayenne pepper
2 cups milk
2 eggs
1 small green cabbage, outer leaves removed, cut into 8 wedges (leave the core intact to hold leaves together)
Canola oil for deep frying
Salt to taste
Grated Parmesan cheese to taste

Whisk together flour, cornstarch, salt, garlic, cumin, paprika, thyme, oregano, and cayenne in a mixing bowl.

Whisk together milk and eggs in a second bowl.

Dredge each cabbage wedge in the flour mixture; shake off excess. Dip into milk mixture; let excess drip off. Return wedges to flour mixture; shake off excess.

(continued on next page)

Transfer prepared wedges to a baking sheet and repeat the process with remaining wedges. Chill the baking sheet of wedges.
Heat 2-1/2–3 inches of oil in a large pot (at least 6 inches tall) to 375 degrees.

Carefully add two wedges to the pot and fry until the cabbage is tender and golden brown, 3–5 minutes. Adjust heat as needed to maintain the oil temperature of 350 degrees.

Transfer fried wedges to a plate with a few paper towels on it to drain any excess oil. Repeat frying with remaining wedges.

Season the fried wedges with salt and Parmesan cheese.

Arrange wedges on a serving platter in a round starburst design. Enjoy with your favorite dipping sauce.

Serves 8.

Bacon Cabbage Dippers

3 medium green cabbages
3 pounds bacon
3/4 cup grated Parmesan cheese
6 tbsp extra-virgin olive oil
Kosher salt and ground black pepper
3 tbsp smoked paprika
3 tbsp brown sugar
3 tbsp dried oregano
3 tbsp garlic powder
3 tbsp onion powder

Preheat oven to 450 degrees F.

Cut the cabbage in half and remove the thick stem. Cut each half into four wedges.

In a bowl, mix Parmesan, salt, pepper, paprika, brown sugar, oregano, garlic powder and onion powder.

Brush each wedge with oil and coat with the Parmesan mixture, then wrap each wedge in a piece or two of bacon.

Arrange the cabbage on two large baking sheets. Bake until cabbage is golden and crispy around edges and bacon is cooked through, about 30 minutes.

Serve warm with ranch for dipping or your favorite sauce.

Makes 24 servings.

PICKLED, RELISHES & SALSA

Basic Sauerkraut

1 medium green cabbage, cored, sliced very thin
1 tbsp sea salt

Place the sliced cabbage in a large bowl. Add the salt. With very clean hands, massage the salt into the cabbage, firmly squeezing the cabbage as you work. Keep this up for at least five minutes, ten is even better. The cabbage will release liquid, which is what you want it to do.

Jam the cabbage into a quart size sterilized canning jar. Push hard to pack it in as tightly as you can. When the jar is full of cabbage, carefully pour the salty liquid that was extracted from the cabbage into the jar until all the cabbage is covered. If there is any leftover liquid, put it in a covered container and set it aside for now.

Drape a clean cloth or plastic wrap over the jar and secure it with a rubber band. Set the jar in a dark, cool place.

For the next three days, press down on the cabbage twice a day, and add more of the liquid as needed. The cabbage should always be submerged.

After three days, taste the sauerkraut. If it's to your liking, put a lid on the jar and keep it in your refrigerator.

You can enjoy the sauerkraut right away, or let it continue maturing in the refrigerator for the next two to three weeks, if you prefer.

Pickled Red Cabbage

1/4 small red cabbage, cored and shredded
1/2 cup apple cider vinegar or red wine vinegar
1/2 cup water
1 tbsp white granulated sugar
1 clove garlic, minced
1 tsp salt
1/4 tsp pepper

Place all ingredients in a mixing bowl, stir until blended.

Spoon the blend into a large glass jar and put the lid on finger tight.

Leave the jar on the kitchen counter for three to six hours, occasionally shaking up or stirring the contents.

Store the sealed jar in the refrigerator. The pickled cabbage will be good for at least two weeks.

Absurdly Easy Kimchi

2 napa cabbages, cored, rinsed, cut in 2-inch squares
1-1/4 cups coarse sea salt
1 tbsp fish sauce
5 green onions, chopped
1/2 small white onion, minced
2 cloves garlic, pressed
2 tbsp white sugar
1 tsp ground ginger
5 tbsp Korean chili powder

Place cabbage into large Ziploc bags and sprinkle the salt as evenly as possible over the leaves. Rub the salt into the cabbage squares. Zip the bags shut and let them sit out at room temperature for 6 hours.

Transfer the cabbage squares to a colander and rinse thoroughly with cold water to remove the salt. Squeeze the squares to drain out excess liquid.

Place rinsed cabbage in a large mixing bowl and stir in fish sauce, green onions, white onion, garlic, sugar, and ginger. While wearing protective gloves, sprinkle Korean chili powder over the mixture and rub it into the vegetables until they are evenly coated.

Transfer the mixture into a large glass container with a well-fitting lid. Seal the lid finger tight and let it rest quietly for four days in a cool dry place. Refrigerate before serving. Will keep in the refrigerator for up to a month.

Cabbage Salsa

1 small green cabbage, cored and finely chopped
1 cup Campari or grape tomatoes, diced
1/2 bunch cilantro including stems, chopped
1/3 cup pickled jalapeños, chopped
2 tbsp jalapeño pickling liquid
1 garlic clove, grated
4 tbsp lime juice
1 tbsp orange juice
2 tbsp white vinegar
Salt to taste

Combine all ingredients in a bowl and mix well. Refrigerate for at least a half hour before serving.

Roma tomatoes may be substituted, but keep in mind that they will not be as sweet as Campari or grape tomatoes.

Chopped parsley may be substituted if you are among those who have a genetic aversion to cilantro.

Beet Relish for Canning

14-16 medium beets
1 small green cabbage
1 large white onion
2 red bell peppers
1-1/2 cups white granulated sugar
1 tbsp kosher salt
4 tbsp horseradish, finely minced
3 cups white vinegar

Clean and peel the beets.

Chop or coarsely grind the beets, cabbage, onion and peppers.

Place all ingredients in a large pot. Bring to a boil and cook for ten minutes.

Fill hot, sterilized jars, leaving 1/2 inch of headspace. Remove air bubbles. Add more relish if the headspace dropped. Wipe rims with a towel dipped in hot water, place hot lids on jars, screw ring on snugly.

In a boiling water bath, process half pints for 15 minutes or pints for 20 minutes.

Garden Melody Corn Relish

8 cups sweet corn kernels
4 cups green cabbage, chopped
1 cup white onion, chopped
1 cup green bell pepper, chopped
1 cup red bell pepper, chopped
1 cup white granulated sugar
2 tbsp ground dry mustard
1 tbsp celery seed
1 tbsp mustard seed
1 tbsp salt
1 tbsp turmeric
4 cups apple cider vinegar
1 cup water

In a large saucepan, combine all ingredients. Bring to a boil.
Reduce heat and simmer 20 minutes.

Pack warm relish into clean jars with well-fitting lids. Store
in the refrigerator.

If you wish to can your relish, process pints or jelly jars for
15 minutes in a boiling water canner.

SALADS

Magic Ramen Salad

*"So easy, a child could do it; so cheap,
a college student can afford it."*

1 small green cabbage, finely chopped
2-3 green onions, chopped
1 package quick ramen noodles, crumbled
1/3 cup peanut oil
1/3 cup cider vinegar
1/3 cup white granulated sugar
1/4 tsp curry powder
1 clove garlic, finely minced
Flavor packet from ramen noodles (any flavor)

In a mixing bowl, combine cabbage, green onions, ramen noodles.

In another bowl, combine peanut oil, cider vinegar, sugar, curry powder, garlic, and the flavor packet. Mix thoroughly to create a dressing.

Pour the dressing over the vegetable/noodle mixture. Stir well to blend, cover the bowl and refrigerate overnight.

The noodles will soften to make an unusual pasta salad.

Cabbage & Noodles Salad

3 cups green cabbage, shredded
1 package quick ramen noodles, crumbled
1/4 cup sunflower seeds, shelled and roasted
1 tsp onion, minced
Flavor packet from ramen noodles (any flavor)
1 tbsp white granulated sugar
2 tbsp white vinegar
1/4 cup water
1 tbsp olive oil

In a mixing bowl, combine cabbage, uncooked ramen noodles, sunflower seeds and onion.

In another bowl mix the contents of the ramen flavor packet, sugar, vinegar, water and olive oil. Pour this wet mixture over the cabbage mixture.

Cover bowl and refrigerate until the noodles are tender.

Sweet & Sour Cabbage Salad

Rumors in my family say that this salad will stay crisp for up to two weeks, but it's always been devoured in a couple of days, so I can't vouch for that.

1 large green cabbage, grated
1 large green bell pepper, seeded and grated
1 large white onion, grated
1/2 cup honey
2/3 cup olive oil
2/3 cup white vinegar
1/2 cup white granulated sugar
1 tbsp salt

Grate the cabbage, green pepper, and onion into a large bowl and set aside.

In a saucepan, add the honey, olive oil, vinegar, sugar and salt. Bring the mixture to a boil, then turn off the heat and let it cool.

Mix the cooled sauce with the grated vegetables.

Store in an airtight container in the refrigerator.

SLAWS

Ken's Favorite Coleslaw

3/4 cup mayonnaise
1/3 cup sour cream
1/4 cup white granulated sugar
3/4 teaspoon seasoned salt (I use Lawry's)
1/2 teaspoon ground dry mustard
1/4 teaspoon celery salt
1 small green cabbage, finely chopped
1/2 cup red cabbage, finely chopped
2 large carrots, peeled and grated
6 large radishes, grated
1/4 cup white onion (Vidalia is preferred), finely diced

In a large bowl, combine mayonnaise, sour cream, sugar, seasoned salt, mustard, celery salt. Mix until well blended into a dressing.

Add the cabbage, carrots, radishes and onion to the dressing and stir to mix thoroughly.

If the dressing is too soupy, shred or mince more of your favorite vegetables. I often add a second carrot or some extra radishes. Keep adding vegetables until the slaw is a consistency you like.

Conversely, if the vegetables aren't coated enough with dressing, add a little more mayonnaise and/or sour cream until you reach a consistency you like.

Refrigerate until ready to serve. Try to eat it as soon as possible while the dressing is still creamy.

Serves 6 regular people, or 2 Kens.

Retro Slaw

8 cups green cabbage, shredded
2 medium carrots, shredded
1 medium green bell pepper, diced
1/2 cup diced white onion
1 tbsp unflavored gelatin
1/4 cup cold water
2/3 cup white granulated sugar
2/3 cup white vinegar
1-1/2 tsp salt
1/4 tsp pepper
2 tsp celery seed
2/3 cup olive oil

In a large mixing bowl, combine the cabbage, carrots, green pepper and onion.

In a small dish, dissolve the gelatin in the cold water.

In a saucepan, bring the sugar, vinegar, salt, pepper and celery seed to a boil. Once at a boil, turn the heat off. Let this dressing cool until it is warm, not hot.

Stir gelatin mixture into the warm dressing in the saucepan. Stir dressing until it has slightly thickened.

Slowly add the oil to the dressing while beating with an electric mixer. Beat for five minutes or until the dressing is well-blended.

Cool dressing completely. Mix dressing with the prepared vegetables and refrigerate overnight in an airtight container.

Stir before serving. Serves 8-10.

Kathy's Cole Slaw for Two

6 tbsp white vinegar
6 tbsp white granulated sugar
4 tbsp olive oil
2 tsp salt
2 cups green cabbage, finely minced
1/2 cup fresh parsley, chopped
1 medium white onion, sliced into rings

In a mixing bowl, blend the vinegar, sugar, oil and salt into a dressing.

Add the cabbage, parsley and onion to the mixing bowl.

Stir to coat all vegetables with the dressing.

Chill for at least two hours before serving.

Serves 2.

Pushcart Coleslaw

1 medium green cabbage, cored and finely shredded
1 medium white onion, diccd
2 large carrots, peeled and shredded
2 cups mayonnaise
1 cup white granulated sugar
1/2 cup apple cider vinegar
1 tbsp salt

Place prepared cabbage, onion, and carrots in a large bowl.

In a separate bowl, blend mayonnaise, sugar, vinegar and salt.

Add the mayonnaise mixture to the vegetables and stir until evenly coated.

Chill slaw. To serve, scoop into paper cones and eat with a wooden spoon while strolling along a boardwalk or lounging on a picnic blanket.

Makes 8-10 servings.

Sara Ramsey Bennett's Cole Slaw

Shared by Sara's granddaughter, Cathy Karas

1/2 medium cabbage, grated
1/3 cup white vinegar
1/2 small green bell pepper, chopped
3 tbsp vegetable oil
2 tbsp white granulated sugar
1 tbsp pimento, chopped
1 tsp dry minced onion
1 tsp salt
1/2 tsp dry mustard
1/4 tsp black pepper
1/2 tsp celery seed

Combine all ingredients in a large bowl.

Serves 12.

Slippery Slaw

6 cups green cabbage, shredded
2 cups carrot, shredded
1 green bell pepper, chopped
1 small white onion, chopped
3/4 cup vegetable oil
1 tsp salt
1/3 cup water
1/3 cup vinegar
1 cup white granulated sugar
1 small package (3 ounces) lemon jello

In a large bowl, mix the cabbage, carrot, pepper, onion and oil.

In a small saucepan, mix the salt, water, vinegar and sugar. Bring to a boil.

When the saucepan is at a boil, add the lemon jello.

When the jello has dissolved, remove the saucepan from the heat and let the mixture cool.

When cool, pour the mixture over the vegetables, stir to blend, and chill until set.

Tossed Salad Slaw

6 tbsp white vinegar
6 tbsp white granulated sugar
4 tbsp olive oil
2 tsp salt
2 cups green cabbage, finely diced
1/2 cup fresh parsley, chopped
1 medium red onion, sliced into rings

Blend the vinegar, sugar, oil, and salt into a dressing. An immersion blender works very well for this, but you can use any method you prefer.

Combine the dressing with the cabbage, parsley, and onion.

Toss lightly until all vegetables are coated with the dressing.

Peg's Favorite Slaw

An Essay Recipe by Peg Betterly Robinson

My personal favorite slaw: Super-fine chop as much cabbage as you think you and your associate eaters are likely to eat. You can shred it fine, chop in a food processor, or do as I do and hand mince it very tiny. The big idea is to get cabbage confetti. Add carrot confetti to taste, if you like.

Toss with about 1/4 tsp salt per cup of chopped cabbage. Place in a plastic bag and allow to sit in the fridge between an hour or so up to a day.

Squeeze the accumulated water out of the bag and toss the squeezed out cabbage into a bowl. Toss with cider vinegar, about a tablespoon per cup of minced cabbage. Drizzle with honey--another tablespoon per cup, more or less. Me, I tend to like a wee bit more--and I add raisins, too.

Finish with mayonnaise and fresh-ground pepper. Check seasoning. If you are me, add just a squeeze more honey.

This slaw can also be made with lemon juice and lemon zest instead of the cider vinegar.

If you are in a rush, you can skip the salt-and-sit marination that lets you squeeze out excess water--BUT! If you do, do not let it sit long: the water will start to ooooze out of the cabbage into the sauce, and it will be runny and wet. Delicious. But runny and wet. So if you want to skip the salt-and-squeeze, then mix everything up and serve within about 15 minutes.

SOUPS & STEWS

Sauerkraut Soup

1 large white onion, chopped
1/4 cup bacon fat
1 tbsp paprika
3 cups sauerkraut, drained and finely chopped
1 clove garlic, crushed
1/4 pound Polish sausage, sliced
6 cups water
Salt and pepper to taste
1 tbsp all-purpose flour
3 tbsp chopped dill
1 cup sour cream, room temperature

In a large saucepan (of a size to hold all ingredients), sauté the onion in the bacon fat over medium heat until just tender.

Remove from the heat and stir in the paprika.

Return the pan to the heat, add in the sauerkraut, and stir with a fork for one minute.

Add the garlic, sausage, water, and season with salt and pepper as desired. Cover the pot and cook on low heat for 30 minutes.

Stir the flour and dill into the sour cream and add the mixture to the soup.

Continue cooking on low heat, stirring often, until the soup is thick and smooth.

Hamburger Vegetable Soup

1 pound ground beef
1 cup russet potatoes, raw, diced
1 cup green cabbage, shredded
4 cups tomatoes: fresh, store-bought, home canned, diced, stewed, whatever is your preference.
3 cups water
1/4 tsp dry basil
1 bay leaf
1 cup white or yellow onion, chopped
1 cup carrots, sliced
1 cup celery, sliced
1/4 cup white or brown rice, uncooked
Salt to taste
1/4 tsp dry thyme

In a frying pan, cook the ground beef and onion until the meat is lightly browned. Drain off the fat.

Add all the ingredients to an adequately sized soup pot and bring it to a boil. Turn down the heat to a simmer and cover the pot. Let the soup simmer for an hour.

Remove the bay leaf before serving.

Red Cabbage & Sausage Soup

2 tbsp olive oil
1/2 white onion, diced
1/2 red cabbage, cored and diced
1 carrot, diced
2 tbsp garlic, diced
3 stalks celery, diced
1 tsp salt
1 tsp pepper
1 tbsp oregano
1 tbsp Hungarian paprika
1 pound smoked kielbasa, sliced
2 cups water
1 bay leaf
3 cups beef broth

In a large Dutch oven or stock pot, heat olive oil. Add onion and cook until soft.

To the pot, add cabbage, carrots, garlic, and celery. Cook until the vegetables are lightly browned.

Season with salt and pepper, oregano, and paprika.

Stir in kielbasa and cook another 4-5 minutes until warmed and lightly browned.

Stir in water, bay leaf, and beef broth. Bring to a rapid boil. Let the soup reduce for about 5-10 minutes.

Remove bay leaf before serving. Serves 6.

Quick Bean & Cabbage Soup

1 tbsp olive oil
1 small yellow onion, diced
3 carrots, diced
1/2 fennel bulb, diced
4 cloves garlic, minced
1 tbsp oregano
1 tsp thyme
1/2 tsp sea salt
1/2 tsp black pepper
1 medium green cabbage, cored and sliced
1 can (approx. 15 ounces) fire roasted tomatoes
1 cup tomato sauce
4 cups chicken broth
1 can (approx. 15 ounces) small white beans, drained and rinsed
1/4 cup fresh parsley, chopped, for serving

Heat olive oil in a large pot over medium high heat. Add onion, carrots, fennel, and garlic. Sauté for 5 to 8 minutes, or until onion is translucent.

Stir in oregano, thyme, salt, pepper, and cook for an additional 5 minutes.

Add cabbage, tomatoes, tomato sauce, chicken broth, and beans.

Bring to a boil, reduce heat to a simmer, cover, and cook for 15 to 20 minutes, or until cabbage is tender.

Garnish soup bowls with parsley. Serves 4.

Poor Man's Stew

1 pound ground beef
1 medium white onion, chopped
2 cups green cabbage, chopped
3 tbsp rice, uncooked
1 can (approx. 1-3/4 cups) condensed tomato soup
1 soup can of water (approx. 1-3/4 cups)

Fry the ground beef and onion, crumbling the beef as it cooks. Drain off any excess fat.

Add the cabbage, rice, soup and water to the meat.

Simmer on medium heat until the rice is cooked through, about a half hour.

Note: If you have a bell pepper of any color on hand, it will make a great addition. Seed and chop it, then add it to the stew in the last ten minutes or so of cooking.

MAIN DISHES

Aunt Julia's Holupki

2 to 3 medium green cabbages
1 large white onion, chopped
3 garlic cloves, chopped
Vegetable oil
2 pounds ground beef, raw
1/2 cup rice (scalded, which is half-cooked)
Salt and pepper to taste
6 oz tomato paste
1 cup water
Sauerkraut (optional)

Cut a deep, wide hole in the stem-end of a cabbage. Drop in a pot of boiling water for 3-4 minutes.

Remove the cabbage from the pot and carefully remove each cabbage leaf. Trim away the thick part of each leaf, lay the leaves out to cool. Save the trimmed-out thick pieces for later.

Fry the onion and garlic in a little oil.

In a large bowl, thoroughly mix together the raw ground beef, rice, salt, pepper, and the cooked onion and garlic. (Note: Save aside a little onion and garlic for lining the pan.)

Prepare a large roasting pan: Add the reserved onion and garlic, tomato paste, water, sauerkraut if desired, salt and pepper to taste. Spread these ingredients evenly over the bottom of the pan.

(Continued on next page)

On the thick end of a cabbage leaf, place ¼ cup of the meat mixture. Roll the leaf towards the thin side. Push the loose ends of the leaf into each side of the roll.

Place the stuffed cabbage leaf in the prepared roasting pan, seam side down.

Keep stuffing cabbage leaves and putting them in the pan until you run out of meat filling. If you need to, you can stack the stuffed leaves in the pan. If you wish, you can add sauerkraut between the layers.

Put the thick pieces of cabbage you saved aside over the top of the stuffed cabbage leaves.

Bake at 350 degrees for about two hours.

These are best if they are left to sit and 'flavor' for at least a half hour after they are removed from the oven. They are even better served the next day.

Holupki For a Crowd

2 medium green cabbages, cored
1 cup white rice, uncooked (do not use instant)
3 cups water
2 medium yellow onions, chopped
3/4 cup (1-1/2 sticks) butter
2 pounds ground beef, raw
1/2 tsp thyme
Salt and pepper to taste
1/2 cup water
2 cups tomato sauce
1 can (1-1/2 cups) condensed tomato soup
1 14 oz can cranberry sauce (jellied style)
2-3 tbsp brown sugar

Boil each cabbage in water for 7 minutes. Remove from pot, then detach each individual leaf and lay them flat. Trim off part of the thick stems on the leaves but do not cut it out. Set aside to cool. Save the bits of stem for later.

Partially cook the rice in three cups of water, just until all the water has been absorbed.

Sautee the onions in the butter.

In a large bowl, thoroughly mix the half-cooked rice, onions, ground beef, thyme, salt, and pepper.

In a large pot, place the pieces of cabbage stems you saved. Lightly salt and pepper them. Add 1/2 cup water, and a spoonful of tomato sauce.

(Continued on next page)

Starting with the largest cabbage leaf, place 1 to 1-1/2 tablespoons of the meat and rice mixture on the leaf, roll tightly and tuck in the sides. Place in pot.

Continue stuffing cabbage leaves, using the largest first for the bottom layers and the smallest for the top. As you complete each layer in the pot, lightly salt and pepper it, and add a bit of tomato sauce.

In a bowl, mix the cranberry sauce, condensed tomato soup and brown sugar. Beat mixture until blended, then pour it over the holupki in the pot.

Cover the top of the holupki stack with any leftover cabbage leaves. Cover the pot with a lid and cook on medium heat until it boils. Then, turn the heat down to low and simmer for 2 hours, or until the top layer of the holupkis are cooked through.

Toltott-Kaposzta
Hungarian Stuffed Cabbage

Just a recipe from "Just George"

1 large green cabbage, cored
1 large white onion
2 tbsp olive oil
½ pound ground beef, raw
½ pound ground pork, raw
1 large egg
2 tsp salt
1 tsp black pepper
1 clove garlic, finely minced
½ cup uncooked white rice, washed
1 cup tomato puree

Place the cabbage in a pot of boiling water. Using a large fork, hold the cabbage underwater. Using a knife, cut loose cabbage leaves as they wilt and remove them from the pot to a cutting board or platter. Keep removing cabbage leaves until they have all been wilted and removed. When the wilted leaves are cool, use a small paring knife to carefully shave away part of the thick stem, but don't cut the stem loose from the leaf. This method will preserve the shape of the leaves. Keep the stem shavings for later.

Chop the onion and sauté it in the oil until tender.

In a large bowl, add the onion, beef, pork, egg, salt, pepper, garlic, and uncooked rice. With your hands, mix everything well.

(Continued on next page)

Chop up all of the leftover cabbage and stem shavings and place it in the bottom of a large pot.

Hold a leaf on the palm of your non-dominant hand. Place a half cup of meat mixture in the center of the leaf. With your dominant hand, fold one side of the leaf over the mixture and roll it up. Tuck in the other side of the leaf gently but firmly.

As each cabbage roll is completed, set it in the pot, on top of the chopped cabbage. As the cabbage rolls fill the pot, arrange them carefully in layers so that they can cook evenly. When they are all in the pot, add cold water to cover them.

Cook on low heat for an hour, or until the rice in the mixture is tender. You will need to do a bit of surgery on a top roll to check if the rice is done.

Serve with a dollop of tomato puree spread over each roll.

Cabbage Unrolls

1-1/2 pounds ground beef
1 large onion, chopped
2 tbsp oil
1/2 cup rice, cooked
1 medium green cabbage, cored and chopped
Salt and pepper to taste
1 can (1-1/2 cups) condensed tomato soup
1 soup can (1-1/2 cups) water

In a skillet, brown the beef and onion in the oil. Remove from heat. Drain any excess oil.

Add the rice to the beef and onion and mix well.

Grease a 9" x 13" baking pan. Add half the cabbage to the baking pan, then add the meat mixture in an even layer, and top with the rest of the cabbage. Season with salt and pepper to taste.

Mix the soup and water. Pour the soup mixture evenly over everything in the baking pan.

Cover the pan with foil and bake at 350 degrees for 1-1/2 hours.

Deconstructed Cabbage Rolls

1 pound ground beef
1 onion, chopped
1 tsp salt
Pepper to taste
1/2 tsp garlic powder
1 tbsp Worcestershire sauce
3 cups green cabbage, coarsely shredded
1 can (1-1/2 cups) condensed tomato soup
1 soup can (1-1/2 cups) of water
3 tbsp white rice, uncooked
1 cup (or more) grated cheddar cheese or cheese slices

In a large frying pan, brown the ground beef. Drain away any fat. Add the onion salt, pepper, garlic powder, and Worcestershire sauce. Cook just until the onions are soft and the ingredients are well blended, about five minutes.

Turn off the heat and add the soup, water and rice. Blend well.

In a casserole pan, spread the shredded cabbage evenly. Ladle the meat mixture over the cabbage. Top the casserole with the cheese.

Cover tightly with foil and bake at 325 degrees for 1-1/2 hours.

Beth's Corned Beef & Cabbage

1/2 cup white onion, chopped
2 tbsp bacon fat
7 cups cabbage, shredded
1 12-ounce can corned beef, crumbled
1/4 tsp pepper
1-1/2 cups water

In a large saucepan, cook the onion in the bacon fat until tender.

Add the rest of the ingredients.

Cover the saucepan and cook on medium heat for 6-8 minutes, or until the cabbage is tender.

Simple Corned Beef & Cabbage

5 pounds well-trimmed corned beef brisket
Water
2 cloves garlic, crushed
1 white onion, quartered
1 medium green cabbage, cut into 8 wedges

Place meat into a large pot and add enough cold water to cover it.

Add the onion and garlic, heat on stovetop until boiling.

Turn down the heat to a simmer and cover the pot. Simmer for 3-4 hours or until tender.

Remove the meat and skim the fat off of the liquid in the pot.

Add the cabbage to the pot and let it simmer uncovered for 15 minutes.

Corned Beef & Cabbage Omelet

3 tbsp oil
2 cups green cabbage, shredded
1 medium red bell pepper, seeded and cut into thin strips
1 small yellow or white onion, sliced thin
8 large eggs
1/4 cup water
2 tbsp Dijon mustard
1 tbsp dill weed, chopped (or 1 tsp dried dill weed)
7 oz corned beef (canned is okay), sliced into 1/2" cubes

In a 10" frying pan, heat 1 tbsp of oil. Add the cabbage, pepper and onion and stir-fry for about three minutes, or until the vegetables are done but still slightly crisp. Remove vegetables from pan into a bowl.

In another bowl, beat the eggs, water, mustard and dill.

In the frying pan, heat 2 tbsp oil. Pour in egg mixture and cook on medium heat until it is set on the bottom. You can check by lifting an edge with a spatula to see underneath.

Arrange all the vegetables and the corned beef on top of the omelet.

Cover the pan with a lid and continue cooking until the omelet is fully cooked, about 8 minutes.

Serves 4.

Meatballs & Cabbage

1 pound ground beef
1 large egg
1/3 cup rice, uncooked
1 medium white onion, finely chopped
Salt and pepper to taste
Vegetable oil for frying
3-4 cups tomato juice
1 small cabbage, either red or green, shredded

Thoroughly mix the raw meat, egg, rice, onion, salt and pepper. Form into small balls.

Brown the meatballs in a little oil in a large frying pan.

Cover the meatballs with tomato juice.

Heap the cabbage on top of the meatballs.

Cover the pan and simmer on low heat for an hour.

Crazy Patties

1 medium green cabbage, cored, sliced into 1" strips
1 32 oz bottle ketchup
1 2-liter bottle ginger ale
2 pounds ground beef
2 large eggs
1 large white onion, chopped well

Place the cabbage strips into an 8-quart stock pot. Pour in all the ketchup and ginger ale. Cover the pot and bring it to a boil, then turn it down to a simmer.

Mix the ground beef, eggs, and onions until well blended. Form the mixture into patties and slip them into the sauce in the stock pot.

Cover the pot again and simmer the patties for 1-1/2 hours.

Serve by scooping some of the cooked cabbage up onto a plate and arranging a patty on top of it.

Dorrie's Pork & Sauerkraut

8 boneless thick cut pork chops or 2-3 pounds pork roast
1 large white onion, diced
1/2 cup butter
Salt and pepper to taste
3 15 oz cans (approx. 6 cups) Bavarian style sauerkraut
3-1/2 cups chicken broth
1 cup brown sugar
8 slices cooked bacon

In a large frying pan, brown meat and onions in butter. Add salt and pepper to taste. Remove meat from pan and set aside.

To the pan, add sauerkraut, broth, sugar and cooked bacon.

Blend ingredients and adjust spices. May need more brown sugar.

Bury the meat in the sauerkraut. Cover and simmer for 3 hours or put it all in a crock pot for 6 hours.

Creamy Pork & Sauerkraut

1 medium white onion, minced
2 tbsp oil
2 pounds pork, cubed
1/2 tsp paprika
Salt and pepper to taste
1/2 cup water
1-1/2 pounds sauerkraut, well drained
1/2 pint sour cream

Fry the onion in oil until browned.

Add the pork, paprika, salt, pepper, and water. Mix well. Simmer on low heat until the meat is cooked through.

Add the sauerkraut, continue cooking until the sauerkraut starts to brown.

Add the sour cream, stir to blend all ingredients, and continue cooking until everything is hot again.

Midwest Sauerkraut Hot Dish

1-1/2 pounds ground beef
1 package (12-16 ounces) wide egg noodles
1 can (1-1/2 cups) condensed cream of chicken soup
1 can (1-1/2 cups) condensed cream of celery soup
3 cups milk
1 large can (28 to 32 ounces) sauerkraut, drained

Fry the ground beef, breaking the meat into crumbles. Drain well.

Cook the noodles according to package directions and drain.

Mix the condensed soups with the milk. A whisk will blend them quickly.

Grease a medium sized roasting pan. Spread the noodles out over the bottom of the roasting pan.

On top of the noodles, arrange the ground beef. Arrange sauerkraut over the ground beef. Pour the soup/milk mixture over everything.

Bake at 375 degrees for one hour.

Middle European Pork & Sauerkraut Roast

1/2 pound bacon, diced
1-1/2 pounds pork, cubed
1 red apple, sliced and cored, peel left on
3 pounds sauerkraut, drained
2 tbsp paprika
1 can beer
1 bay leaf
1 large white onion, diced

Fry the bacon, separating all the pieces as you work, then pour off half the fat.

Add the pork to the bacon, fry for 10 minutes.

Place all the meat in a roasting pan, then add the rest of the ingredients. Stir to mix well.

Bake for an hour at 325 degrees.

Remove bay leaf before serving.

No-Fuss Baked Casserole

1 pound ground beef, raw
2 large eggs
1/2 cup white rice, uncooked
1 cup water
4 tbsp butter, melted
1 small green cabbage, shredded
1 can (1-1/2 cups) condensed tomato soup
2 tbsp brown sugar

In a bowl, mix together the beef, eggs and rice.

In a flat casserole dish, pour in the water and then drip the melted butter randomly over the water.

Scatter half of the shredded cabbage over the water and butter. Drop spoonfuls of tomato soup over the cabbage, using half the can. Spread the meat mixture evenly over the cabbage. Add the rest of the cabbage over the meat mixture. Spoon on the rest of the tomato soup, and lightly sprinkle brown sugar all over.

Cover the casserole dish with foil. Bake at 350 degrees for 1-1/2 hours.

Simple Cabbage Casserole

1 pound ground beef
Salt and pepper to taste
1 medium white onion, diced
1/3 cup rice, uncooked
3 cups cabbage, shredded
1 can (1-1/2 cups) condensed tomato soup
1 can (1-1/2 cups) water

Fry the ground beef, breaking the meat into crumbles.

Add the salt, pepper, onion, and rice to the meat. Heat through.

Mix the soup and water thoroughly.

Transfer the beef mixture to a greased casserole dish.

Spread the shredded cabbage on top of the meat. Pour the soup/water mix over all.

Bake at 325 degrees for two hours.

Virginia's Cabbage Creole

1 pound ground beef or pork
1 medium onion, chopped
1 green bell pepper, seeded and chopped
2 garlic cloves, minced
1 quart diced tomatoes in juice (I use home-canned)
1 medium green cabbage, cored and chopped
1 tbsp chili powder
Salt and pepper to taste

In a large pot or frying pan, brown the ground meat, breaking it into crumbles. Drain away any fat.

Add all the rest of the ingredients, stir to blend.

Cover and cook until the cabbage is tender, about 20 minutes.

Note: Our family enjoys this dish served over rice.

Mom's Quick Fried Cabbage Dinner

I'm going to credit my Mom for this recipe since it was an easy go to dinner for her (who hated to cook!) -- Vicki Shaver

1/2 green cabbage, roughly chopped
1 stick (1/2 cup) butter *Yes, that's how much she put in!! You could half that if you're concerned about that amount of fat.*
Lots of salt and pepper

That's it!

Begin to melt butter in large fry pan over med-high heat. Add chopped cabbage when butter is about halfway melted. Stir fry until crisped to the level you prefer. I like some burnt bits! Add salt and pepper to taste.

Variations include frying 4-6 slices of bacon first, then frying the cabbage in the bacon fat. Mom sometimes snuck in chopped onions, but they didn't agree with Dad, so we were an onion-free household unless she wanted to make two versions of dinner.

Cabbage Pie

1/2 pound ground beef
1/2 cup pizza or spaghetti sauce
1/2 cup margarine
1 cup green cabbage, chopped
4 cups onions, chopped
1/2 tsp salt
1/4 tsp pepper
2 cans refrigerated flaky biscuits
8 ounces mozzarella cheese, shredded

Fry the beef until done, breaking it into crumbles as it cooks. Drain off fat and discard.

Place the meat in a bowl. Stir in the sauce.

In the skillet used to cook the beef, melt the margarine. Add the cabbage, onions, salt and pepper. Cover the pan and simmer over medium heat for 10-15 minutes, or until tender.

In an ungreased 9" x 13" inch casserole pan, place the contents of both biscuit dough cans, evenly spacing the biscuits. With your fingers, press and flatten the raw biscuits until they cover the entire bottom of the pan.

On top of the biscuits, spread the cooked ground beef. Layer the cabbage mixture over the beef, then scatter the mozzarella cheese evenly over the top.

Bake at 375 degrees for 25-30 minutes, or until brown and bubbling. Cut into squares and serve steaming hot.

Lori's Fast Fish Tacos

I keep a box of store-bought crunchy corn taco shells in the cupboard and frozen breaded fish sticks in the freezer for nights when we need a fast dinner. Stirring up a batch of coleslaw pulls it all together.

6 crunchy pre-folded corn taco shells
12 breaded fish sticks
2-3 cups coleslaw (mayonnaise based, not vinegar based)

Bake the fish sticks per package directions.

Chop the fish sticks into roughly 1" pieces.

Fill the taco shells with a layer of fish stick pieces and top each one with a big dollop of coleslaw.

Enjoy!

This recipe is based on our favorite way to make a quick dinner, but you are welcome to use any sort of fish you like, breaded pieces or whole filets, fresh or frozen. Just make sure the fish is thoroughly cooked and any inedible skin is removed. Break your cooked fish into chunks or leave filets whole.

These are free-form tacos, so do whatever appeals to you and your family.

Soft tortillas, either corn or flour may be substituted. You could also try filling a pita pocket.

Kids LOVE these.

SIDE DISHES

A Bubble & Squeak Tutorial

Bubble and Squeak is a traditional British food made from leftovers, typically those from a Sunday roast dinner. The dish dates back to at least the 18th century. The name comes from the sounds that come from the pan while the dish is being fried.

Traditionally, the main ingredients are potatoes and cabbage. Leftover vegetables, as well as leftover roast meat, bacon, or ham can be included.

If using leftover potatoes, they are often mashed or roughly chopped. The cabbage and any other vegetables are finely chopped or shredded.

Combine the potatoes and vegetables in a mixing bowl. Season with salt and pepper.

Heat a generous amount of oil or butter in a frying pan. Add the mixture and press it down with a spatula, or if you wish, you can form the mixture into patties for easier flipping.

Cook on medium heat until the bottom is browned and crispy. Flip the mixture or patties to cook the other side until crispy.

Bubble and Squeak is often served as a side dish, but it can be a main course when meat is included. With eggs on the side, it makes a fine breakfast, too.

Irish Colcannon

2 pounds potatoes, well-scrubbed. If very large, cut in half.
1/2 cup butter
5 ounces Canadian bacon, chopped
1 small Savoy cabbage, shredded
2/3 cup heavy cream

Place the potatoes in a large saucepan of water. Bring to a boil and simmer for 15-20 minutes, or until they are fork tender.

Meanwhile, heat half the butter in a saucepan, then fry the bacon and half of the cabbage for five minutes. Turn off the heat and set aside.

Drain the potatoes in a colander and peel them while they are still hot. Mash the potatoes until smooth.

In a small saucepan, warm the cream with the rest of the butter to almost boiling.

Beat the cream into the potatoes. Add bacon and cabbage to potatoes and mix to blend. Season with salt and pepper to taste.

Bacon Substitutes: Sliced back bacon is a good choice for the United Kingdom and Europe. Center-cut bacon might be easier to find in some regions in the USA.

Scottish Rumbledethumps

2 pounds russet potatoes, peeled and chopped
6 tbsp butter – divided into 3 tbsp portions
2 small white onions, sliced
1 Savoy cabbage, roughly sliced
Salt and pepper to taste
1 cup cheddar cheese, grated

Boil the potatoes for 15-20 minutes or until tender. Mash them with 3 tbsp butter and season them with salt and pepper to taste.

Fry the onions until softened; set aside.

Fry the cabbage in the remaining butter until it has softened and wilted down in the pan.

In a large bowl, blend the potatoes, cabbage and onion.

Put the mixture into an ovenproof dish.

Top with grated cheese and bake at 350 degrees for 15-20 minutes or until the cheese has melted and turned golden brown.

Serves 6.

Indian-ish Cabbage

An Essay Recipe by Peg Betterly Robinson

One small or half a medium or large onion, PLUS half a head of garlic, PLUS about 1-2 inches of ginger, peeled, then zizzed up in a mini-processor or mashed in the mortar with just enough water to keep it from jamming up.

Sauté the resulting paste in butter, ghee, or oil until tawny. Add 2 TBSP cumin, 2 TBSP coriander (seed, ground), 1/4 tsp nutmeg, 1 tsp fennel, fry long enough to heat spices and toast them nicely.

Add approximately 4 cups very finely shredded cabbage, and sauté till tender, adding small amounts of oil and/or water If needed.

This is now a base for a variety of Indian-ish ways to go. You can add just a bit of broth and a heap of chopped parsley and serve as a wet vegetable side. You can add yogurt. You can add cream. You can add cream and tomato paste. You can add cream and tomato paste and queso blanco. You can add cream and curry powder. You can add cream and garbanzo beans. You can garnish all of these options with chopped fresh cilantro.

The big trick is just to sauté the original heap of fine-sliced cabbage with classic Indian onion-ginger-garlic paste, and then add things that look harmonious to moisten and sauce the result. Keep it simple and it's very hard to go wrong.

Sweet & Sour Cabbage

1 large yellow onion, chopped
Butter or oil for frying
1 medium green cabbage, cored and cut into ½" slices
1 can (1-1/2 cups) condensed tomato soup
1 soup can (1-1/2 cups) water
1/2 cup raisins
Salt to taste
2 tbsp lemon juice
1 tbsp granulated white sugar

Brown the onion in butter or oil.

Place all ingredients into a stock pot. Bring it to a boil, then turn it down to a simmer.

Cook until the cabbage is tender and the flavors have blended.

Cheesy Cabbage

1 medium green cabbage, cored and cut into 1-inch slices
1 cup bread crumbs (or Panko)
1 tbsp Italian herb seasoning
1 stick (1/2 cup) butter or margarine
Salt and pepper to taste
1-1/2 cup milk
8-10 slices of Velveeta cheese (or 2-1/2 cups shredded cheddar cheese.)

Place cabbage in a pot of boiling water for 8-10 minutes, drain.

Mix the bread crumbs or Panko with the Italian herb seasoning.

In a casserole dish, spread out a layer of cabbage. Sprinkle some of the seasoned bread crumbs over the cabbage. Cut small pieces of butter and scatter them on the bread crumbs. Season to taste with salt and pepper.

Repeat the layers (cabbage, bread crumbs, butter, salt and pepper) until you use up these ingredients.

In a small saucepan, warm the milk and cheese until it is blended and melty. If needed, you can add a little more milk.

Slowly pour the cheese sauce over the top of the casserole.

Bake at 350 degrees until the top starts to brown, about an hour.

Cabbage Fritters

1 small green cabbage, shredded
2 small carrots, shredded
2-3 green onions, thinly sliced
2 cloves garlic, finely minced or crushed
3 large eggs, slightly beaten
4-5 tablespoons all-purpose flour
1 teaspoon sea salt
1/2 teaspoon black pepper
1/2 teaspoon paprika
2-3 tablespoons avocado oil for frying

Mix the cabbage, carrots, green onions, and garlic in a large mixing bowl.

Add the slightly beaten eggs to the mixing bowl, along with the flour, salt, pepper, and paprika. Mix thoroughly. You may use your hands if you wish.

Preheat a large skillet over medium heat. Once the pan is hot add a couple tablespoons of avocado oil. Let the oil heat for a minute.

Using an ice cream scoop or your hands, form a ball about the size of your palm, place it on the skillet, and press down with a spatula until the fritter is about 1/4 an inch in thickness.

Fry the fritters for 3-4 minutes on each side until they are a deep golden-brown color.

Serve warm with sour cream or your favorite sauce.

Cabbage Parmesan

1/3 cup plus 2 tbsp canola oil, divided
1 large green cabbage
2 tsp kosher salt
4 cloves garlic, grated
1 tbsp chopped fresh basil, plus more for serving
1 cup marinara sauce
1/2 cup Pecorino Romano or Parmesan, finely grated
8 1/4" slices fresh mozzarella
Extra-virgin olive oil for drizzling

Preheat oven to 425 degrees. Line a baking sheet with foil. In a large skillet over medium-high heat, heat 1/3 cup oil.

Cut two ends off cabbage, then cut cabbage lengthwise into four 1" to 1-1/2" thick slices. Carefully cut out core, making sure to keep slices intact.

Arrange slices in skillet and season with salt. Depending on their size, you may need to cook slices individually. Cook, turning occasionally, until golden brown on both sides, 6 to 7 minutes. Transfer to prepared baking sheet.

In a small bowl, mix garlic, basil, and the remaining 2 tablespoons oil. Brush top of cooked cabbage slices with this mixture. Spoon 1/4 cup marinara sauce on each cabbage slice and sprinkle with Pecorino Romano. Top with 2 slices mozzarella.

Bake cabbage until cheese is bubbly, 18 to 20 minutes.

Arrange cabbage on a platter. Drizzle with olive oil and top with basil.

Cabbage & Comforts

8 oz wide egg noodles
4 tbsp oil
3 cups russet potatoes, cut into 1/2 inch cubes
1 cup chopped yellow onion
6 cups cabbage, shredded
1/2 cup chicken broth
1/2 tsp thyme
Salt and pepper to taste
1 large tomato, seeded and chopped

Cook noodles in boiling water until tender; about 5 minutes. Drain and set noodles aside.

Heat the oil in a Dutch oven or large pot with a cover, on the stovetop on medium heat. To the pot, add the potatoes and onions. Cover and cook 5-7 minutes.

Stir in cabbage, broth, thyme, salt and pepper. Cook 8-10 minutes, or until vegetables are tender.

Stir in the noodles and tomato and heat through.

Homemade Potato Noodles
with Cabbage

1 medium green cabbage, shredded
1 tsp salt
4 tbsp margarine
2-3 tbsp sugar
2/3 cup plain mashed potatoes
2 large eggs
2 cups all-purpose flour
1/2 tsp salt

Note: More salt will be needed for a pot of boiling water; I've listed two measurements of salt in the ingredients as it is also used in measured amounts in the recipe.

Put the shredded cabbage in a colander set over a bowl. Sprinkle it with 1 tsp salt and let it stand for about 15 minutes. With your hands, squeeze the cabbage firmly to press out the juice.

In a heavy skillet, melt the margarine and add the cabbage. Cook over low heat, stirring often, for about a half hour or until cabbage is very soft.

Add the sugar to the cabbage and stir to blend.

In a mixing bowl, add the mashed potatoes, eggs, flour and 1/2 tsp salt. Knead the potato mixture well. Add more flour if needed to form a dough.

(Continued on next page)

Roll the dough out on a floured surface until it is 1/8 inch thick. Cut the dough into 2" wide strips.

Dust flour over the strips, then stack 3 strips on top of each other. Repeat till all strips are stacked.

Using a knife, cut through the stacks the long way to make noodles. You can make wide noodles with just one slice or cut thinner strips if you prefer.

Drop the noodles into a pot of boiling water that has been salted (this is the third use of salt in this recipe).

Boil until the noodles rise to the surface. Drain them in a colander, rinse them with hot water, drain again.

Lightly mix the noodles with the cabbage.

Quick Fried Cabbage & Noodles

1 small green cabbage, chopped
2 tbsp oil or bacon grease
1 small white onion, sliced
1/2 cup water
4 cups wide egg noodles, cooked and drained
Salt and pepper to taste

Add the oil or bacon grease to a large frying pan.

Add the cabbage and onion to the pan and fry until tender.

Add the water, cover the pan and let it simmer for a few minutes.

Remove cover, add the noodles, salt and pepper.

Stir to blend all ingredients and cook until everything is warmed through.

DESSERTS

Julie's Sweet Haluski

1 cup uncooked wide egg noodles
1/2 cup butter
4 cups cabbage, finely chopped
1 tsp salt
3 tbsp white granulated sugar
1/4 tsp cinnamon

Cook the noodles per package directions, drain well, then cut them into little squares.

Melt the butter in a heavy saucepan. Add the cabbage, salt, sugar, and cinnamon.

Cook over low heat for about 30 minutes, stirring often, until cabbage is soft and browned.

Serve in small bowls as a sweet and savory comfort food.

Cabbage Strudel

First, make "Julie's Sweet Haluski" - the recipe on the previous page. This will be used as your strudel filling.

Parchment paper
10 sheets phyllo dough, at room temperature
1/2 cup butter
Julie's Sweet Haluski

In a small saucepan, melt the butter.

Place a sheet of parchment paper on a baking sheet with the narrow end closest to you, and top with a sheet of phyllo dough.

Brush the phyllo dough with butter. Top with another sheet of phyllo, and brush again with butter. Repeat until all 10 sheets are buttered and stacked.

Arrange the sweet haluski on top of the dough stack, along the narrow side that is closest to you, in a 2" thick, even layer.

With the aid of the parchment paper, roll the cabbage layer and phyllo dough stack. Roll carefully, making sure not to trap the parchment paper in the roll. Keep rolling until all the cabbage and phyllo dough is an enclosed tube. Discard the parchment paper.

Brush top of the roll with butter, place on baking sheet and bake until golden brown, about 40 minutes.

Sauerkraut Surprise Cake

1/2 cup butter
1-1/2 cup granulated sugar
3 large eggs
1 tsp vanilla
2 cups all-purpose flour
1 tsp baking powder
1 tsp baking soda
1/4 tsp salt
1/2 cup cocoa powder
1 cup water
1 8-oz can sauerkraut, drained, rinsed, and finely minced.

In a large mixing bowl, cream the butter until smooth. Beat in the eggs, one at a time. Add vanilla.

In another bowl, mix the flour, baking powder, baking soda, salt, and cocoa powder. Slowly add the dry ingredients to the creamed mixture, adding a little of the water each time, until all the dry and wet ingredients are well blended. Stir in the sauerkraut.

Grease and flour a 13"x9"x2" baking dish and turn the batter into it. Bake at 350 degrees for 35-40 minutes, or until an inserted toothpick comes out clean.

When cool, frost with Sour Cream Chocolate Frosting. The recipe is on the next page.

Sour Cream Frosting
for Surprise Cake

6 oz semi-sweet chocolate chips
4 tbsp butter
1/2 cup sour cream
1 tsp vanilla
1/4 tsp salt
2-1/2 to 2-3/4 cups powdered sugar

Melt the chocolate and butter in a pan over very low heat. When smooth, turn off the heat.

To the chocolate mixture, add the sour cream, vanilla and salt. Blend well.

Gradually beat in powdered sugar until desired consistency is reached.

Still Hungry?

Pick up volume one in the "Brassbright Cooks" series!

Steamed and Steamy
Recipes from the Steampunk World of Industralia

"Even fictional characters gotta eat. These are their recipes. Now you can make the favorite foods of the fictional country of Industralia, from breakfast right on through to late night snacks. You'll even learn how to make traditional New Year's "Coal Week" holiday treats."

What foodies are saying about Steamed and Steamy

"Ah, the delightful sounds and smells of cooking. And explosions. Or maybe that is just my kitchen… Venture forth into the wilds of your own kitchen to explore the possibilities for flavor and ingredients you encountered in your explorations of Industralia! From carnival peanuts and cotton candy to some hearty meat pies these recipes can help you, or a young friend, cook some of the flavors of adventure." – Nurseferatu

"At our house, "Coal Cookies" have become a holiday tradition for little steampunks and not-so-naughty children. Brass-bright bon appetit! – Susan L. Fox

"I really felt like I'd met characters from a small town, even though it was an imaginary place I'd never visited! The practicality and down-home quality of the recipes appealed to me." – Jami Good

"Buy this along with *The Flight to Brassbright*. Then you'll have the delight of a steampunk novel full of delightful and memorable characters to read AND a book of recipes to go with it!!!" – B. Koslowski

"Written by one of the steamland's best wordsmiths, this is a great book to add to your collection!" – BlakOpal

"I adore this book! The recipes are wonderful and the stories are funny, inspiring, and entertaining." – D. Hartigan

"Great recipes and the steampunk lore is fun. The candyfloss is brilliant." – Simon Howard

Steamed and Steamy is available in paperback or eBook online everywhere. Books2Read will guide you directly to it at your favorite bookseller.

books2read.com/SteamedAndSteamy

About the Author

Lori Alden Holuta lives between the cornfields of mid-Michigan, where she grows vegetables, tea mints, and herbs, when she's not playing games with a cat named Chives. She's fond of activities from the past, including canning and preserving, crocheting, and cooking.

At her website, "A License to Quill" you can learn more about her writing, editing, book reviews, and just for you foodies, don't miss her recipes and 'Living Simply' articles!

Visit "A License to Quill" at
ceejaywriter.com

Books by Lori Alden Holuta

The Brassbright Chronicles

The Flight to Brassbright

Brassbright Kids

Full Steam Ahead
A Short Story Collection Where Kids Save the Day

Brassbright Cooks

Steamed and Steamy
Recipes from the Steampunk World of Industralia

Shredding It
A Cabbage Cookbook

Where To Find Lori's Books

brassbrightcity.com

books2read.com/LoriAldenHoluta

Subscribe for monthly updates at
brassbrightcity.com/newsletter